weebee Series Three
(Books 17 – 24)
Complete Resource Book

Published by:
Crossbridge Books
Worcester

© R M Price-Mohr 2021

All rights reserved. No part of this publication may be reproduced, stored in a retrieval system or transmitted in any form or by any means – electronic, mechanical, recording or otherwise – without prior permission of the copyright owner.

Permission is given to photocopy the resource pages.

ISBN 978-1-913946-54-8

weebee Series Three Resource Book (Books 17 – 24)

This book contains photocopy-able pages with games and activities designed to support the learning of vocabulary and targeted phonic sounds used in weebee series three (Books 17 – 24). A list of the new vocabulary introduced with each book along with the story text is provided for all books. Lists of the target phonic sounds and high frequency words are also included for each book. The phonic sounds largely follow the 'Letters and Sounds' phonic phases. The high frequency words are from the 250 most common words that comprise approximately 70% of juvenile reading. A handbook and other resources can be downloaded free of charge from the website: https://crossbridgeeducational.com

Instructions for Series Three Games

Books 17 to 20 have a game called 'LexiLudum'. This original game was created uniquely for the weebee Reading Scheme using the theory of Systemic Functional Grammar developed by Michael Halliday (see An Introduction to Functional Grammar third edition, 2004). Using the vocabulary found in the books, players create sentences assembled according to their grammatical function. Sentence holders are provided for two players but can be photocopied for multiple players. Dice with coloured sides are needed (purple on two opposite sides, blue on two opposite sides and yellow on the two remaining opposite sides as shown in the image below).

Sentence holders are made by folding the sheet in half, then folding up the white edge, then folding it back in half again so that it stands up with a shelf at the front and the colours visible. The words in coloured squares need to be cut out and laid on the table, grouped according to their colours. Players take it in turns to roll coloured dice. If they have a space of the colour that they have thrown they can select a word. They will need two purple cards, one yellow and one blue to make a sentence. The winner is the first person to complete three sentences.

Books 21 to 24. For these books, there are additional words on green cards that are conjunctions. For this you will need one of the faces on the dice to be coloured green (use one of the yellow faces). Each player now needs two sentence holders so that they can make longer sentences of two clauses joined by one conjunction (green card). The winner is the first player to complete two sentences of two clauses.

Contents:	Page
Book 17 (At the bridge) word list, targeted phonics, high frequency words and text	4
LexiLudum	6
Phonics sheet (_ain)	14
Book 18 (Into the unknown) word list, targeted phonics, high frequency words and text	16
LexiLudum	18
Phonics sheet (_ight)	22
Book 19 (The journey begins) word list, targeted phonics, high frequency words and text	24
LexiLudum	26
Phonics sheet (_oat)	30
Book 20 (The strange pond) word list, targeted phonics, high frequency words and text	32
LexiLudum	34
Phonics sheet (_alk)	38
Book 21 (Following the trail) word list, targeted phonics, high frequency words and text	40
LexiLudum Extended	42
Phonics sheet (_ing)	52
Book 22 (Lucky escape) word list, targeted phonics, high frequency words and text	54
LexiLudum Extended	56
Phonics sheet (_ide)	62
Book 23 (The rescue) word list, targeted phonics, high frequency words and text	64
LexiLudum Extended	66
Phonics sheet (_ear)	72
Book 24 (The journey home) word list, targeted phonics, high frequency words and text	74
LexiLudum Extended	76
Phonics sheet (_ound)	82
Pupil Tracking Sheet	84

At the bridge 17

Word list:

autumn	telling	rubbing	noisy	us
leaves	about	their	yes	buttercup
turning	friends	legs	please	made
grasshopper	messages	together	river	chain

Targeted phonics:

au-
_ain
_oi_
_ou_

High frequency words:

us
about
their
made

Text:
1. It was autumn and the leaves on the trees were turning brown. A grasshopper had come for a chat with Grog.
2. The grasshopper was telling Grog about all his friends. "They can send messages by rubbing their legs together." he said.
3. Pip came to see the grasshopper. He looked very big to her. When he rubbed his legs together it was very noisy.
4. When the grasshopper had finished rubbing his legs together, he hopped away to find his friends. "It must be fun to hop like that," said Grog.
5. "Can you come for a walk with me?" Pip asked Grog. "Yes," said Grog "where do you want to go?"
6. "Can we go back to the bridge please?" asked Pip. "Yes," said Grog "I like the bridge. We can look at the river."
7. "Can we see if Mop wants to come with us?" asked Grog. "Yes," said Pip "We can all go together." They went to find Mop.
8. Mop was playing with a buttercup. She had made a buttercup chain. "Do you want to go for a walk with us?" asked Grog. "To the bridge," said Pip. "Yes please," said Mop.
9. The friends walked across the field. Mop took her buttercup chain with her.
10. On the way across the field they saw the troll. He wanted to go back to the bridge with them. "Can I come with you? he asked. "Yes," said Pip.
11. When they got to the bridge, the troll jumped up on the wall.
12. Mop wanted to play with her buttercup chain. She wanted to swing from the bridge. "This is fun," she said.
13. "Please can I have a go?" asked Pip. "Yes," said Mop. But Pip went into the water. She was scared.
14. Her friends looked for her on the river, but they could not find her. "We must go and find her," said Grog.

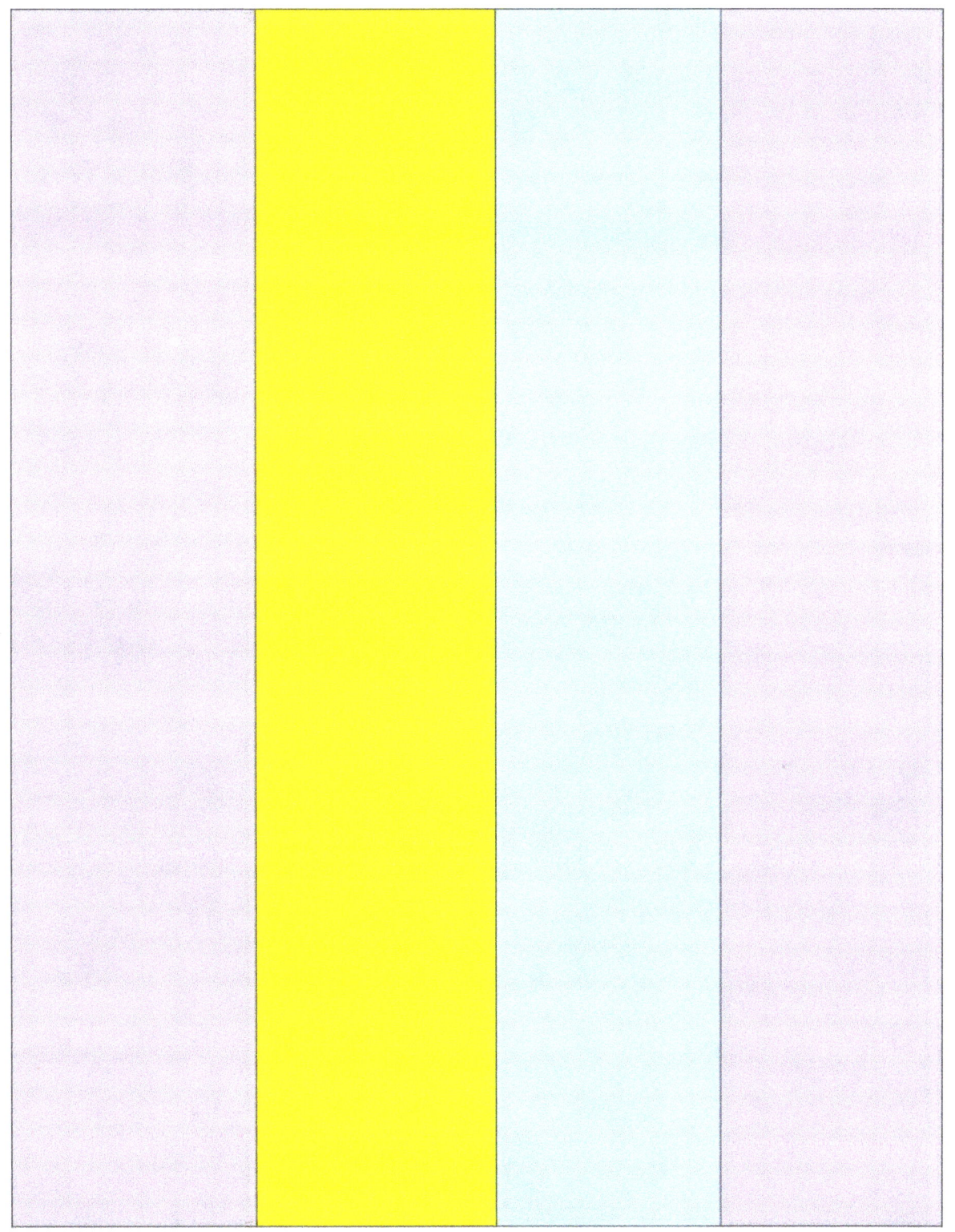

LexiLudum Sentence Holder 1

the chick	made a noise	together with	the egg
the caterpillar	was rubbing	next to	the legs
the duck	said yes	about	the frog
Saff	flew	by	the mushroom
Flup	had a chat	in	us
Tod	said please	and went to	the butterfly
the dragon	sent messages	to	their friends

Book 17 LexiLudum Sheet 1

Grog	was turning	back to	the bridge
the grasshopper	hopped	onto	the autumn leaves
Mop	walked	across	the chain
Pip	was getting	over	the buttercup
the troll	jumped	into	the river
Zon	was telling	about	the tree
Jig	was noisy	down by	the pond

Cut along bold lines and feed through the window

Into the unknown 18

Word list:

landed	past	fast	last	found
floated	hole	round	bank	after
along	bend	tight	who	letting
know	still	reeds	mouse	ground

Targeted phonics:
- _ight
- _oa_
- _ee_
- _ou_

High frequency words:
- fast
- last
- found
- round
- after
- who
- know

Text:
1. Pip had been lucky. She had landed on a little twig that floated along the river. But she was very scared. She did not know where she was going.
2. The twig floated past a lily pad. Pip could see a friendly frog, but the twig was going too fast.
3. Next Pip went past some long grass. She could see a friendly duck, but the duck did not see her.
4. Then the river went round a bend. Pip was still going very fast. She had to hang on tight to the twig.
5. At last, the twig floated into some long reeds. Pip could get off the twig at last. She jumped onto the riverbank.
6. On the river bank, Pip saw a hole that looked as if it was a nest. Pip peeped into the hole to see who was there.
7. It was a friendly mouse. "Please can I come in for a rest?" asked Pip. "Yes," said the mouse, "have you come a long way?" "Yes," said Pip "and I don't know the way home."
8. "Once, when I was very small, I got lost. I was very glad when my mother found me," said the mouse. "Who will try to find you?" asked the mouse. "I am sure my friends will look for me," said Pip.
9. After her rest, Pip went on her way. "Thank you for letting me rest in your nest," she said to the mouse. Pip walked to some tall trees. It looked dark in the woods.
10. The sky was getting dark. Pip could see the moon and some stars twinkling. There were brown, yellow and red leaves on the ground.
11. Pip wanted to find somewhere to sleep. She looked under a mushroom but there was an ant's nest.
12. Pip looked into a hole in a tall tree, but there was a spider on its web.
13. Pip saw a bug. "Can you help me?" she asked. But the bug just flew up into a tree.
14. Then Pip found somewhere to sleep. She did not know what it was, but it was soft and dry.

the mouse	went	past	the bank
the stick	floated	along	the bend
the duck	could stay	tight on	the reeds
Saff	landed	by	the hole
Flup	looked	for	the box
Tod	went fast	round	the tree
the dragon	found it	on	the ground

Book 18 LexiLudum Sheet 1

Grog	had to be still	after	the bridge
the frog	wanted to	know	the message
who	went	across	the lily pad
Pip	was last	over	the bridge
the troll	jumped	into	the river
Zon	is letting her	go after	the duck
Jig	went fast	round	the bulrushes

Cut along bold lines and feed through the window

The journey begins 19

Word list:

fallen	other	called	met	hope
tried	should	can't	boat	take
which	why	how	let's	may
gone	because	another	space	collect

Targeted phonics:
    _oat
    wh_
    _ll_

High frequency words:
    other
    should
    take
    which
    why
    how
    may
    because
    another

Text:
1. When Pip had fallen into the river, Grog and Mop tried to find her. They did not know which way she had gone.
2. Grog, Mop and the troll went to find the other weebees to see if they could help. "We should try to find the grasshopper," said Grog. "Why?" asked Mop. "Because he can send a message," said Grog.
3. When they got back to the big tree, Grog called for Jig. She flew down to see what he wanted.
4. "Pip has fallen into the river and we can't find her," said Grog. "How can I help?" asked Jig. "If you can find the grasshopper, he can send a message for us," said Grog.
5. When the grasshopper came, Grog asked him to send a message to his friends. "Can you ask them if they have seen Pip," said Grog.
6. A message came back for the grasshopper. "A frog saw Pip float by on a twig," said the grasshopper. Then he got another message. "She met a mouse on the river bank," said the grasshopper.
7. "We need a boat to float down the river to the mouse," said Mop. "Yes, the mouse can tell us which way Pip has gone," said the troll.
8. "How can we make a boat?" asked Jig. "Let's ask Zon to help," said Grog. They went to find him.
9. "If I help you make a boat, will you let me come with you?" asked Zon. "Yes, we can all go together," said Grog.
10. Zon found his old space ship. He took the foil door from his shell to mend the space ship. "I hope it will float," he said.
11. "We will need some help to take this to the river," said Grog. "I will go and find the others," said Jig.
12. They all helped to take the boat to the river. Jig, Flup and Saff collected some food.
13. Grog asked Mop and the troll to stay at home. "Pip may come back before use," he said.
14. They put the boat onto the river and it did not sink. Grog, Zon and Tod got into the boat and floated down the river.

the mouse	walked	past	the boat
Grog	tried to	collect	the leaves
Pip	called	to another	duck
Tod	had fallen	into	the river
Flup	should look	for	the other box
because Tod	met him	in	space
why did Pip	hope	for	the boat

how did Tod	take it	across	the bridge
which frog	hopped	onto	the lily pad
Mop may	walk	across	the bridge
let's	go	into	the woods
the troll	has gone	into	the river
Zon	can't find	another	boat
Grog	can skip	under	the trees

Cut along bold lines and feed through the window

The strange pond 20

Word list:

woke	tail	purple	hid	strange
noise	top	suddenly	pile	croaked
inside	first	thing	talk	understand
bird	would	huge	same	more

Targeted phonics:
  _alk
  _oi
  _ir
  _ur

High frequency words:
  top
  first
  thing
  bird
  would
  more

Text:
1. It was still dark when Pip woke up. When she looked up she could see a tall orange hill. She could hear a scary noise from inside the hill. Pip ran back to the trees.
2. On the other side of the trees, Pip could see some big rocks. She hoped to see the way home from the top of the rocks.
3. When Pip got to the top of the highest rock, she could see a long way. She could see a pond. She wanted to see if it was her home.
4. First, Pip would have to go across a green field. There were tall purple flowers in the field. A butterfly saw Pip going past the purple flowers.
5. Suddenly, Pip saw something in the grass. It looked like a huge monster. Pip was very scared. She hid by a rock.
6. The monster went under a pile of leaves. Pip quickly ran past the pile of leaves and went on her way.
7. When Pip came to some tall trees, she found a pile of nuts on the ground. She saw something high up in the tree. It looked like a mouse with a long fluffy tail.
8. Pip kept walking. It was a long way to the pond. She did not know if it was her pond. It did not look the same.
9. When Pip got to the pond, she could see that it was not the same as her pond. First she found some strange flowers.
10. Next she saw some strange frogs. "Do you know where Grog is?" Pip asked the first frog. But he just croaked, he did not understand her.
11. Pip kept walking until she saw some more strange frogs. "Do you know where the oak tree is?" she asked one of them. But he just croaked, he did not understand.
12. Pip walked past some strange ducks. She did not want to talk to them.
13. Pip was upset. She did not know the way home. She did not like the strange pond.
14. At last she found somewhere to rest. But suddenly a huge bird came to take her to his nest.

the frog	hid	inside	a strange box
the bird	flew	up to	the tree
the frog	croaked	at	Tod
the purple frog	did not	understand	Zon
Zon	would not	talk to	the mouse
Tod	went first	into	the field
Pip	suddenly	met	a huge frog

Grog	found more	under	the thing
Mop made	a noise	on top of	the box
Pip	woke up	by	the lily pad
Pip	looked	at	the pile
the huge troll	hid	under	the same bridge
the tail	went	into	the hole
Saff	saw	over	the pile

Cut along bold lines and feed through the window

Following the trail 21

Word list:

held	your	didn't	hopeless	broken
rushing	morning	never	might	claws
soon	our	shall	clue	cliff
there	through	it's	helped	idea

Targeted phonics:
- _ing
- _aw
- _igh

High frequency words:
- your
- morning
- never
- soon
- our
- there

Text:

1. Grog, Tod and Zon held on tight as their boat went rushing round a bend.
2. Soon the boat crashed into the river bank. Pip's twig was still there. "Look, it is the same twig," said Zon.
3. The friendly mouse peeped out of her hole. "Are you looking for your friend?" she asked. "Yes, we are looking for our friend Pip," said Grog. "Have you seen her?" asked Zon.
4. The mouse told them that she would show them which way Pip had gone in the morning. "It's too dark now. You can sleep here," she said.
5. In the morning the mouse showed them the way to the dark wood. They walked round the wood until they came to the pile of rocks.
6. They didn't know which way Pip had gone. Just then Flup saw a butterfly. It was the butterfly they had helped. The butterfly told Flup that she had seen Pip going through the field.
7. The friends went through the field but they didn't know which way to go. Saff flew high in the sky. She could see the small pond. "Let's try looking by the pond," said Grog.
8. Tod tried asking the strange frogs if they had seen Pip but they didn't understand him. They just croaked back at him. Tod was upset "We will never find her," he said.
9. "What shall we do?" asked Zon. "It's hopeless," said Tod. Grog asked Jig, Saff and Flup to fly high over the pond. "You might find a clue," he said.
10. Just then, a robin flew up from a tree. It was the robin they had helped mend its broken wing. Jig asked the robin if he had seen Pip.
11. The robin said he had seen something small and pink in the claws of a big bird. "Where did the big bird come from?" asked Grog. "The big birds nest on the cliffs by the big hills," said the robin.
12. "What shall we do?" asked Tod. "I have an idea, but we will need the robin to help us," said Grog. "I will help you if I can," said the robin.
13. "We need to collect some of the big leaves that have fallen from the trees," said Grog. They made the leaves into a flying boat.
14. "I hope this works," said Tod. The robin, Saff, Jig and Flup flew up in the air and up went the flying boat.

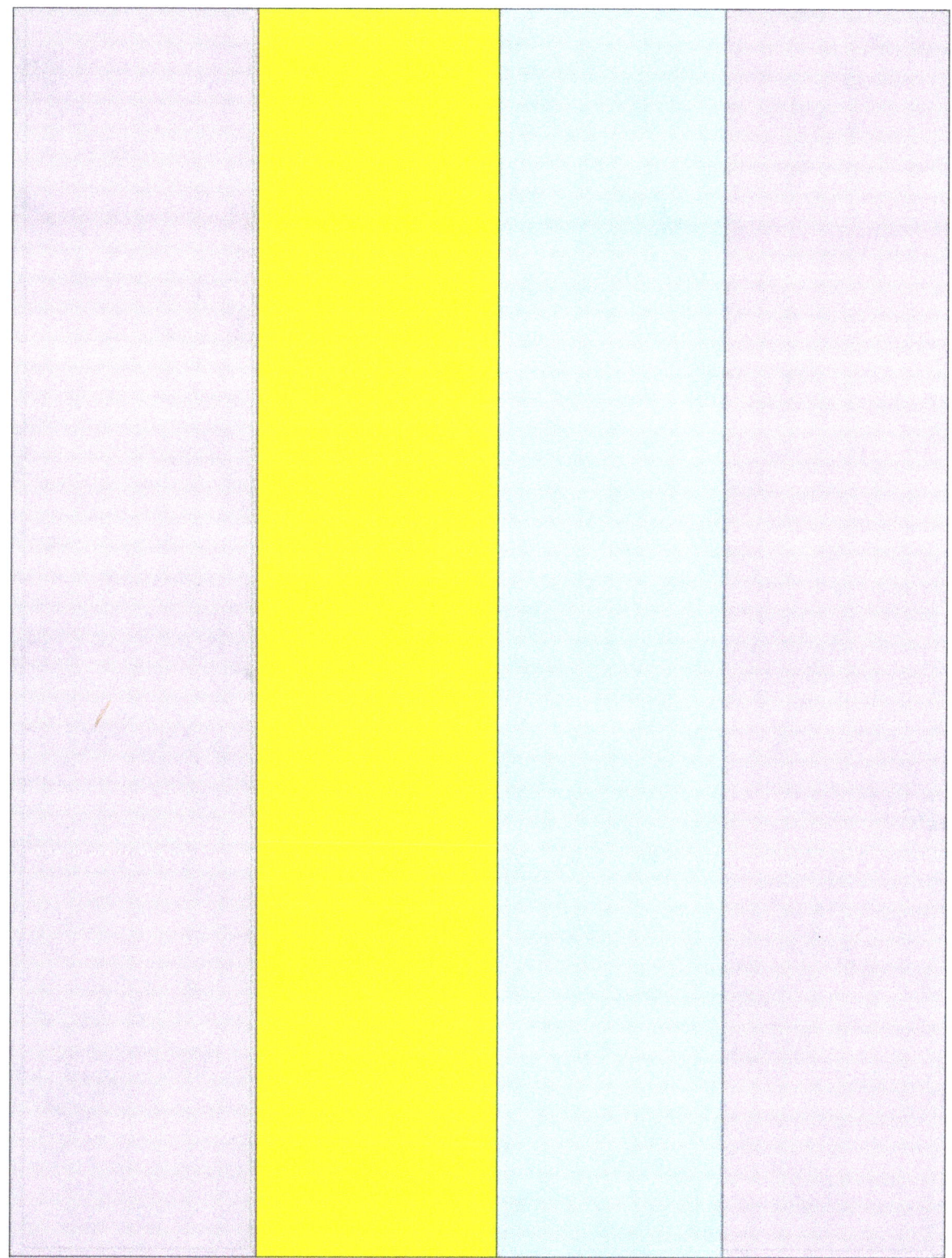

LexiLudum Sentence Holder 3

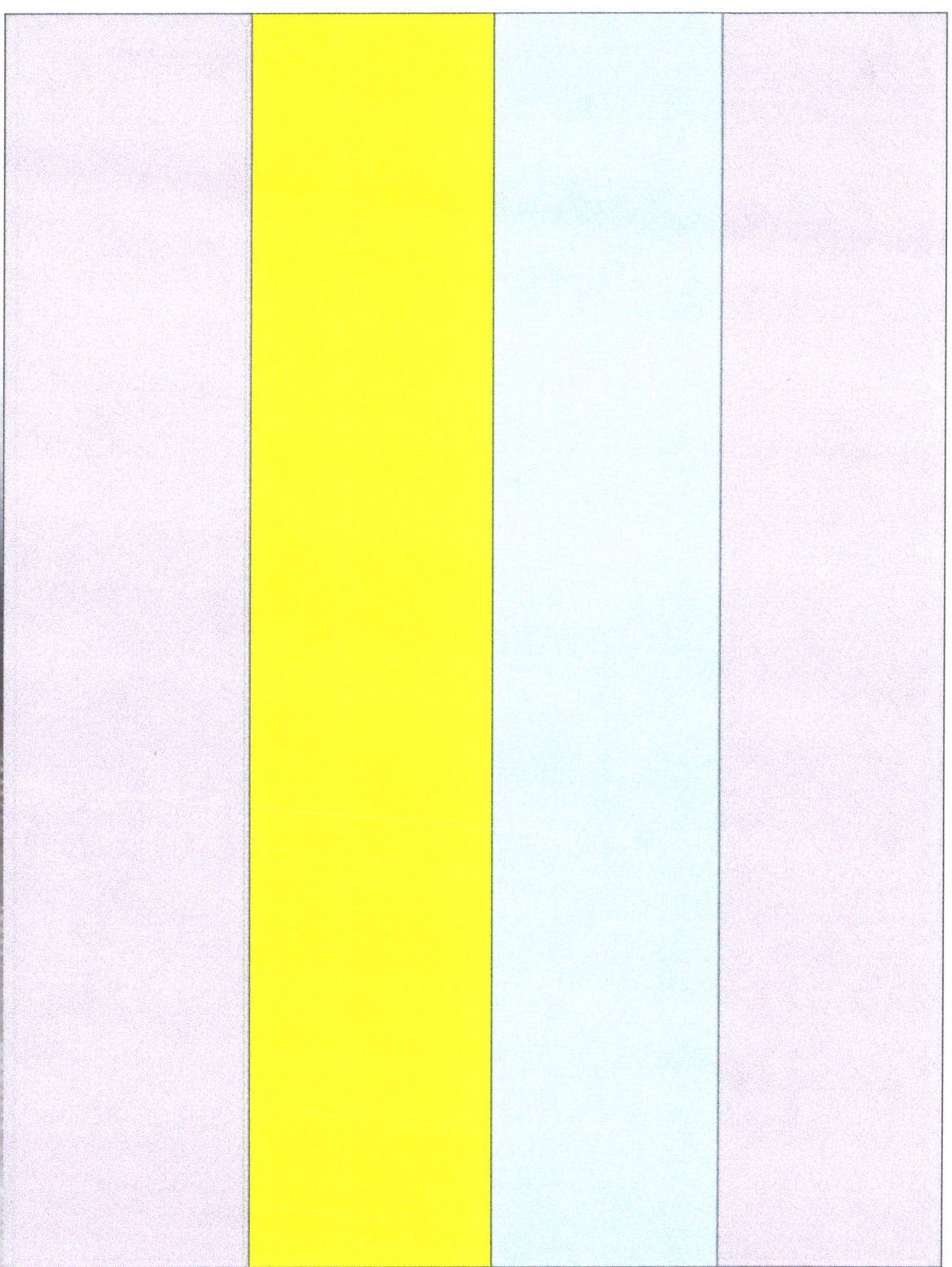

and	but	so	for
after	as	as if	so long as
because	before	then	so that
and then	until	what	when
and	but	then	or
as soon as	as well as	how	if
and soon	that	where	next

Grog	saw it	by	the cliff
the bird	put her	in	his claws
Jig	helped	with	the broken twig
Saff	didn't	find	the clue
Flup	helped	with	the idea
Tod	held	onto	the twig
it's hopeless	he said	through	the trees

Grog	might go	rushing into	the woods
the troll	never went	over	the bridge
your friends	soon went	down	our hole
Pip	went out	in	the morning
the butterfly	shall go	into	there
Zon	crashed	into	the reeds
Saff	flew	across	the sky

Cut along bold lines and feed through the window

Lucky escape 22

Word list:

poor	herself	below	every	away
different	taking	any	escape	flown
thought	began	dropped	edge	hide
colour	still	move	gave	lucky

Targeted phonics:
  _ide
  _dge
  _ow

High frequency words:
  every
  away
  any
  gave

Text:
1. Poor Pip found herself hanging from the bird's claw. The bird flew high up in the air. Pip could see the pond below her. It looked very small.
2. The big bird flew over the top of the tall trees. Everything looked different from up in the air. Poor Pip was very scared.
3. Pip didn't know where the bird was taking her. She didn't know what the bird wanted to do with her. She didn't want any big birds to eat her.
4. Soon Pip could see some tall cliffs. She could see other big birds in their nests. "I need to escape" she thought to herself.
5. Pip could see some small strange flowers near the nest. The flowers were pink. "If I could get under them I could hide from the big bird" thought Pip.
6. Pip began to swing. It hurt her ear but she kept swinging. When the bird dropped her into the nest, she landed on the edge.
7. Quickly, Pip jumped down and hid under the pink flowers. The big bird could not see Pip any more because she was the same colour as the flowers.
8. Pip kept very still. She did not move. Soon the bird gave up looking for her and flew away.
9. Pip peeped out from under the flower. She could see that the bird had flown away. She didn't want another bird to get her. She took a flower to hide under.
10. Pip quickly jumped down the cliff. The other birds didn't see her. "I am going to escape," she thought to herself.
11. Pip could not see the pond next to the cliff. She could not see the pond because it was under some tall trees.
12. Suddenly, Pip saw an owl. It had seen Pip jumping down the cliff. Pip thought the owl was going to get her. Now she could see the pond. Pip was scared because she didn't know how to swim.
13. Suddenly a big leaf landed on the pond. "That was lucky," thought Pip as she jumped onto the leaf. The leaf floated across the pond. Pip could see a hole by the root of a tree.
14. Pip jumped off the leaf and hid in the hole. The owl could not see her and flew away. "That was a lucky escape," thought Pip to herself.

and	but	so	for
after	as	as if	so long as
because	before	then	so that
and then	until	what	when
and	but	then	or
as soon as	as well as	how	if
and soon	that	where	next

Grog	was scared	of	the cliff edge
the bird	had flown	away from	the pond
Pip	could see	below	the trees
poor Pip	found herself	on the edge of	the cliff
Zon	dropped	below	the tree
lucky Tod	escaped	by	the hole
Pip	gave flowers	to	the butterfly

Grog	went to hide	under	the tree
the owl	was taking every thing	from	the nest
Mop	thought	about	the flower
Pip	began to move	through	the air
Tod	kept still	by	the rock
the colour	was different	in	the pond
Saff	didn't see any thing	up in	the sky

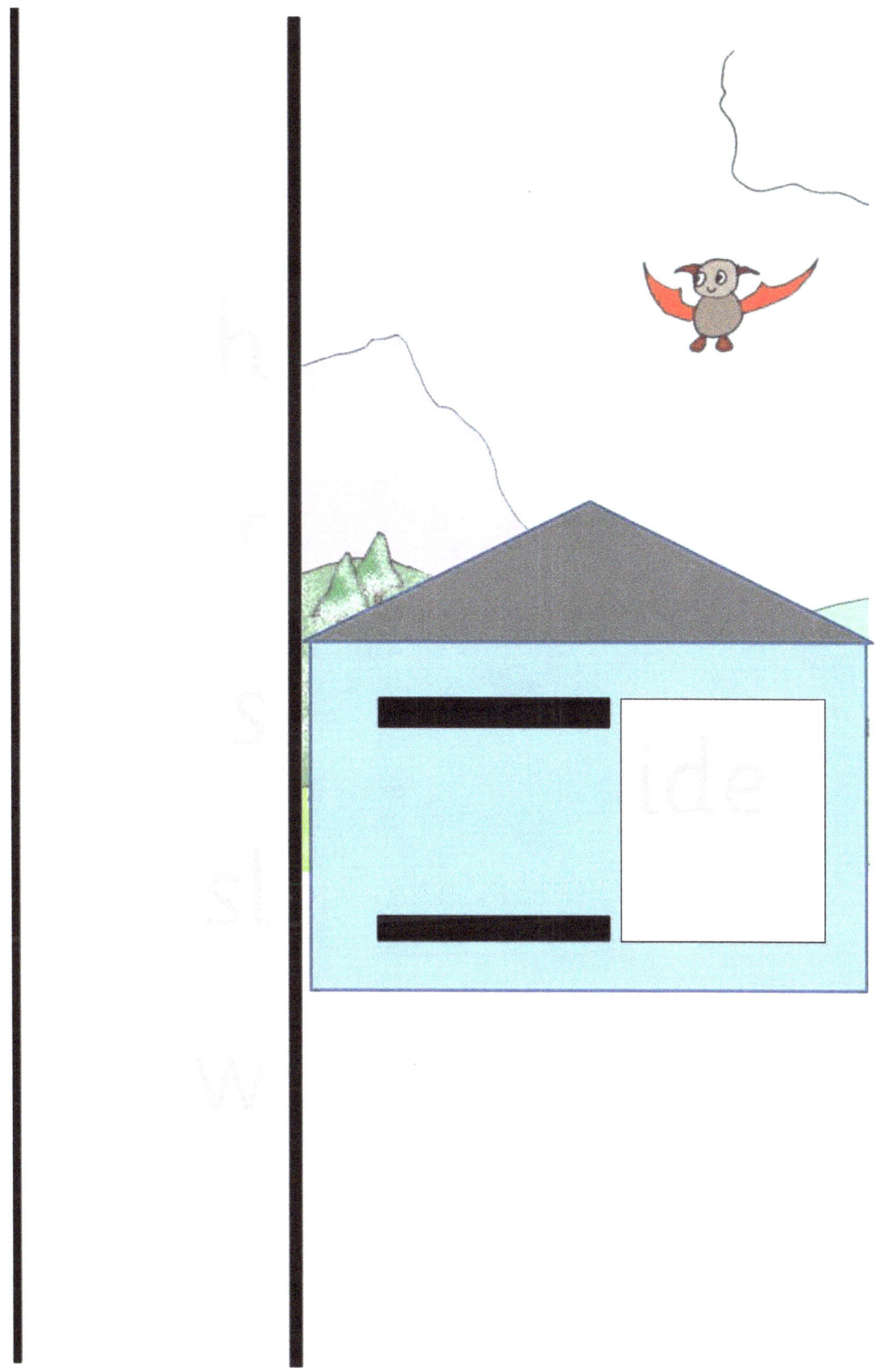

Cut along bold lines and feed through the window

The rescue 23

Word list:

taken	worried	bottom	catch	shouted
think	near	tired	toys	far
somewhere	lower	many	rested	tomorrow
safe	place	give	swooped	night

Targeted phonics:
- _ear
- _tch
- _ight
- _oy

High frequency words:
- think
- toy
- far
- many
- give

Text:

1. Grog, Tod and Zon looked down from the flying boat. They could see small trees below them. They looked like toys. "I do hope we don't fall," said Tod.
2. "How will we find Pip?" asked Zon. "We don't know which nest she has been taken to," said Tod. "I think we should try to land somewhere safe first," said Grog.
3. When they saw the tall cliffs, Grog was worried. "We must not land near the nests. It will not be safe," said Grog.
4. "Let's fly lower and look for a safe place to land," said the robin. "Look there is a pond at the bottom of the cliffs," said Flup. "We can land near the edge of the pond," said Zon.
5. The flying boat landed at the edge of the pond. Jig, Flup and Saff were very tired from flying. They needed to rest. "Thank you for your help," said Grog as the robin flew home.
6. Zon looked up at the cliffs. "There are too many nests, we will never find Pip," he said sadly. "We can't give up now," said Tod.
7. "We could fly up and have a look," said Jig. "It's not safe, the big birds might catch you," said Grog. "We could fly to the top of a tree and look from there, "said Saff. "Yes, that should be safe," said Grog.
8. After they had rested, Saff, Jig and Flup flew up to the top of a tree.
9. Suddenly, an owl swooped down out of the sky. "Look out!" shouted Grog. "Quick, under the mushroom," shouted Tod.
10. They hid under the mushroom until the owl had gone. "I think we are safe now," said Grog. Zon didn't want to come out. "It's safe now," said Tod.
11. Flup flew down from the tree. "We can't see Pip. We are too far away," he said. Grog looked up at the sky. "It's getting dark, we will have to look for her tomorrow," he said.
12. "We need a safe place to stay for the night," said Tod. Zon pointed to a hole in an old tree. "Look, there is a safe place to stay," he said.
13. The friends quickly ran to the hole in the tree. "Look, it's Pip!" shouted Zon.
14. Pip woke up and saw all her friends. She was very, very happy to see them.

when	which	and then	before
after that	but	so	and turning
only	until	and said	suddenly
and soon	and poor	luckily	somewhere
and rushing	next	and looking	then shouted
but then	because	quickly	strangely
inside	together	noisily	slowly

Grog	rested	below	the cliff
the bird	went far	away from	his nest
Jig	wanted to	give	the egg
Saff	found herself	safe in	the lake
Flup	was worried	about	tomorrow
Tod	sat	near	the toys
Pip	was lower	than	the place

Grog	was tired	somewhere by	the tree
many birds	swooped	after	the owl
Mop	shouted	at	the bottom
Pip	needed to think	about	the night
Tod	was taken	into	the tree
Zon	wanted	to catch	the bird
Saff	walked	across	the pond

Book 23 LexiLudum Sheet 2

Cut along bold lines and feed through the window

The journey home 24

Word list:

storm	shelter	spring	toe	carry
struck	phew	wire	washed	strong
lightning	sound	nails	new	wait
stream	thunder	ouch	enough	time

Targeted phonics:
_ound
_ight
_ew
_oe

High frequency words:
new
time

Text:
1. There was a flash in the sky. "Oh! What was that?" asked Pip. "It must be a storm. We are not safe in the tree. It might get struck by lightning," said Grog.
2. "Where can we go?" asked Pip. She was scared of the storm. "We saw a stream on the other side of the pond. We might find somewhere safe near the stream," said Saff.
3. The friends went out into the rain. They were getting wet. Suddenly, Tod saw something to shelter under. "Look, we can shelter under there," he shouted. "Phew, I thought we would be washed away," said Pip.
4. There was an old wooden box to shelter under. "How are we going to get home?" asked Pip. "We don't know which way to go," said Tod sadly. "Or how far it is," said Flup. There was another flash of lightning and the sound of thunder. "We need help," said Grog.
5. Zon looked at all the things on the ground near them. "I think I have an idea," he said. "We can put some of the things together to send a signal. The lightning will help," he said.
6. The friends collected an old spring, some wire, some nails and some wood. As Zon banged the things together, he hit his toe. "Ouch! My toe!" he shouted. "Let me help," said Grog.
7. When it was finished they put it out in the rain. "We can send a signal when the lightning flashes," said Zon. The lightning flashed but it didn't work. "Put it next to a tree and try again," said Grog.
8. When the lightning struck again, it sent a signal. Far away on Zon's planet the robot saw the signal. Quickly he got into his space ship to fly down to look for Zon.
9. It was not long before the robot found the weebees. "We can't all fit into the space ship," said Pip. "We need a new idea," said Jig. "Zon, can you ask the robot to find the dragon's mother? She is big enough to carry us all home," said Grog.
10. The robot took off again and flew away. "I do hope he finds her," said Flup. "We are not strong enough to carry you all home," said Jig.
11. They had to wait a long time. The storm finished. In the morning they looked up at the sky. "Look, I can see something red in the sky!" shouted Zon. Now they could all see the dragon far away. They could hear the sound of her huge wings.
12. The dragon was very happy to help the weebees. She was strong enough to carry them all.
13. It didn't take long for the dragon to fly them home. Soon they saw the big tree and the pond. Mop and the troll were there.
14. "We were very worried," said Mop. "We had to wait a long time," said the troll. They were all very, very happy to be home. They all sat down for a happy picnic.

when	which	and then	before
after that	but	so	and turning
only	until	and said	suddenly
and soon	and poor	luckily	somewhere
and rushing	next	and looking	then shouted
but then	because	quickly	strangely
inside	together	noisily	slowly

Grog	sheltered	from	the storm
the robot	flew	away from	the sound
Jig	washed it	in	the stream
Saff	was scared	by	the thunder
the lightning	struck	on	the wire
Tod	had enough	of	the wire
Pip	wanted	to carry	the spring

she	wanted	to find	the nails
a frog	jumped	onto	his toe
Mop	said phew	to	Tod
he	said ouch	to	the mouse
Tod	found it	by	the strong box
Zon	waited	to catch	the new toy
they	waited	for	a long time

Cut along bold lines and feed through the window

Pupil Tracker			
Name:			
Book	Activity	Date of 1st occurrence	Date of 2nd occurrence
17	LexiLudum		
	Phonics sheet		
18	LexiLudum		
	Phonics sheet		
19	LexiLudum		
	Phonics sheet		
20	LexiLudum		
	Phonics sheet		
21	LexiLudum Extension		
	Phonics sheet		
22	LexiLudum Extension		
	Phonics sheet		
23	LexiLudum Extension		
	Phonics sheet		
24	LexiLudum Extension		
	Phonics sheet		

www.ingramcontent.com/pod-product-compliance
Lightning Source LLC
Chambersburg PA
CBHW080252170426
43192CB00014BA/2658